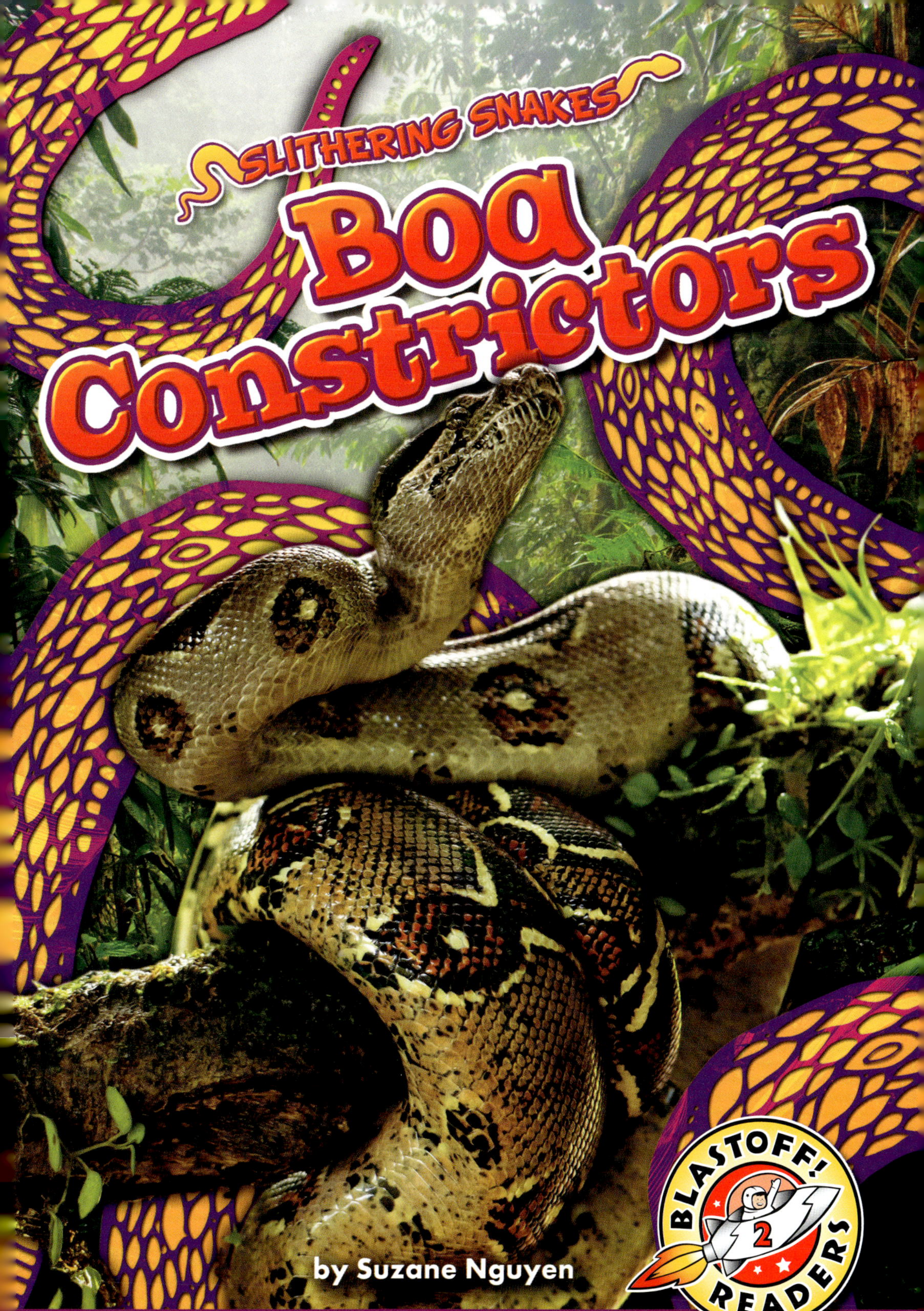

Slithering Snakes

Boa Constrictors

by Suzane Nguyen

Blastoff! Readers 2

BELLWETHER MEDIA • MINNEAPOLIS, MN

Blastoff! Readers are carefully developed by literacy experts to build reading stamina and move students toward fluency by combining standards-based content with developmentally appropriate text.

Level 1 provides the most support through repetition of high-frequency words, light text, predictable sentence patterns, and strong visual support.

Level 2 offers early readers a bit more challenge through varied sentences, increased text load, and text-supportive special features.

Level 3 advances early-fluent readers toward fluency through increased text load, less reliance on photos, advancing concepts, longer sentences, and more complex special features.

★ **Blastoff! Universe**

This edition first published in 2025 by Bellwether Media, Inc.

Library of Congress Cataloging-in-Publication Data

Names: Nguyen, Suzane, author.
Title: Boa constrictors / by Suzane Nguyen.
Description: Minneapolis, MN : Bellwether Media, Inc., 2025. | Series: Slithering snakes | Includes bibliographical references and index. | Audience: Ages 5-8 | Audience: Grades K-1 | Summary: "Simple text and full-color photography introduce beginning readers to boa constrictors. Developed by literacy experts for students in kindergarten through third grade"-- Provided by publisher.
Identifiers: LCCN 2024003115 (print) | LCCN 2024003116 (ebook) | ISBN 9798886870350 | ISBN 9781644878798 (ebook)
Subjects: LCSH: Boa constrictor--Juvenile literature.
Classification: LCC QL666.O63 N49 2025 (print) | LCC QL666.O63 (ebook) | DDC 597.96/7--dc23/eng/20240229
LC record available at https://lccn.loc.gov/2024003115
LC ebook record available at https://lccn.loc.gov/2024003116
Library of Congress Cataloging-in-Publication Data

Editor: Betsy Rathburn Designer: Brittany McIntosh

Printed in the United States of America, North Mankato, MN.

Table of Contents

Strong Jaws

Boa constrictors are big **reptiles**.
They have stretchy jaws.
They open wide!

They can be found from Mexico to South America.

Boa Constrictor Range

Boa constrictors usually have brown or tan **scales**. The scales make different patterns. This helps boas blend in!

They have dark stripes near their eyes.

Spot a Boa Constrictor!

Boa constrictors can be over 13 feet (4 meters) long. They can weigh over 100 pounds (45 kilograms).

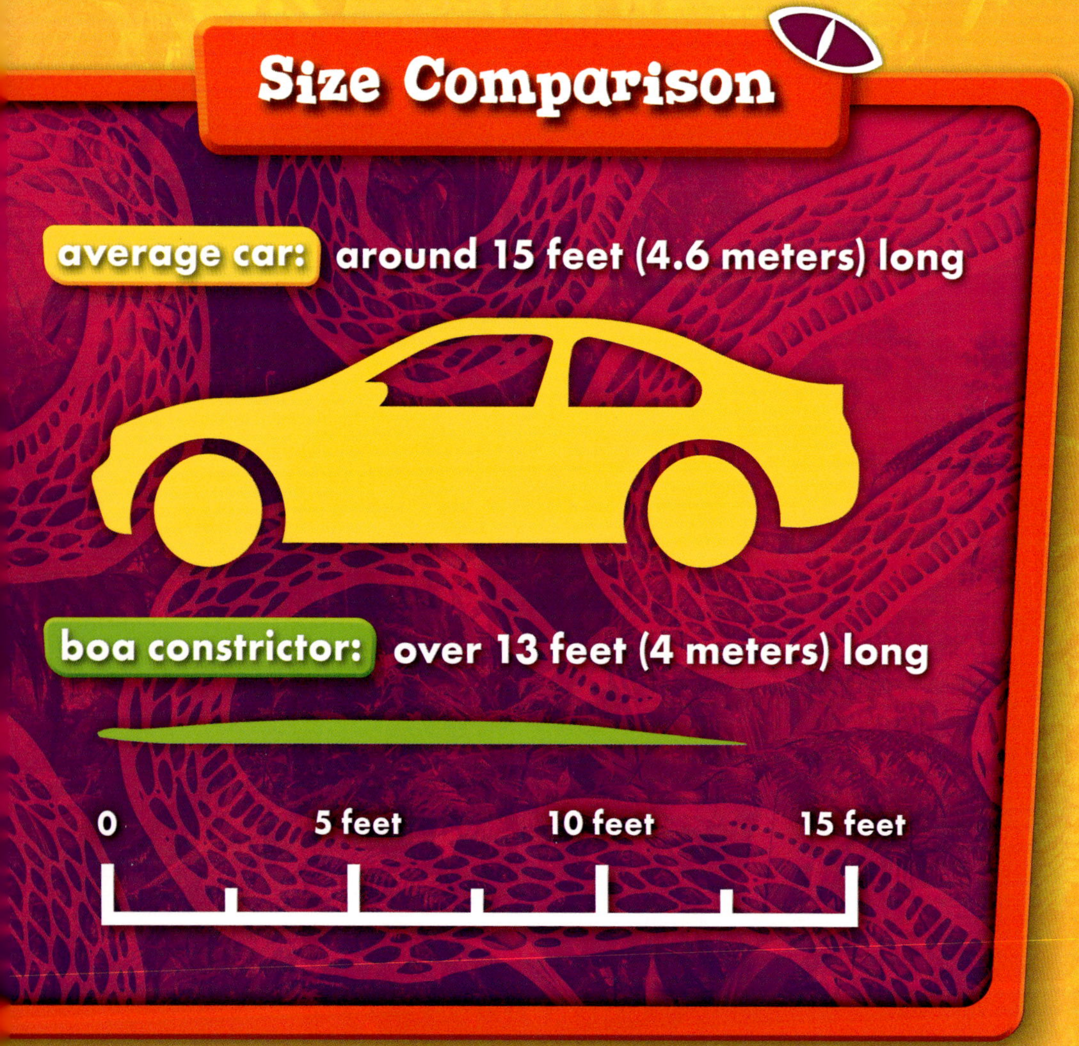

Female boas are larger than males.

Lone Hunters

Boa constrictors live in **rain forests**. They also live in **deserts** and **savannas**.

They spend time in trees. They also hide near streams and rivers.

Boa constrictors are **solitary**. They make homes in logs and animal **burrows**.

They are **nocturnal**.
They mostly hunt at night.

Boa constrictors hide easily.
This lets them **ambush** their **prey**.

When food comes near, they strike! They squeeze prey tightly.

Boa constrictors are **carnivores**. They eat birds, opossums, monkeys, and rats.

Their jaws stretch wide. This lets them swallow prey whole!

Boa Constrictor Food

birds

opossums

monkeys

Young Boas

Female boa constrictors give birth to live young. They have babies about every other year.

They can have over 60 babies at one time!

Baby boa constrictors live on their own right away.

In three or four years, they become adults. They can have their own baby boas!

Boa Constrictor Stats

status in the wild: least concern

life span: up to 30 years

Glossary

ambush—to hunt by lying in wait

burrows—tunnels or holes that some animals use for homes

carnivores—animals that only eat meat

deserts—dry lands with few plants and little rainfall

nocturnal—active at night

prey—animals that are hunted by other animals for food

rain forests—thick, green forests that receive a lot of rain

reptiles—cold-blooded animals that have backbones

savannas—flat grasslands with few trees

scales—plates that cover an animal's body

solitary—living alone

To Learn More

AT THE LIBRARY

Feldman, Thea. *Snakes Smell with Their Tongues!: And Other Amazing Facts.* New York, N.Y.: Simon Spotlight, 2021.

Hicks, Kelli. *Boa Constrictors.* New York, N.Y.: Crabtree Publishing, 2022.

Thielges, Alissa. *Curious About Snakes.* Mankato, Minn.: Amicus, 2023.

ON THE WEB

FACTSURFER

Factsurfer.com gives you a safe, fun way to find more information.

1. Go to www.factsurfer.com.
2. Enter "boa constrictors" into the search box and click .
3. Select your book cover to see a list of related content.

Index

The images in this book are reproduced through the courtesy of: Milan Zygmunt, front cover; J-Re, p. 3; Hemis/ Alamy, p. 4; D. Kucharski K. Kucharska, p. 6; fivespots, p. 7; lunadoc, p. 7 (inset); Karel Bartik, pp. 9, 15, 16, 16-17, 20; Anton_Ivanov, p. 10; Luis Cesar Tejo/ Alamy, p. 11; Roy Palmer, p. 12; Jan Hejda, p. 13; juerginho, p. 14; Fernando Calmon, p. 17 (birds); Celso Margraf, p. 17 (opossums); Edwin Butter, p. 17 (monkeys); Joe Blossom/ Alamy, p. 18; John Cancalosi/ Ardea, p. 19; Alfredo Maiquez, pp. 20-21; New Africa, p. 22.